I0540384

Little Zen Stories

Quiet Teachings for Ordinary Days

Kyra Schaefer

Copyright © 2026 by Kyra Schaefer

ISBN: 978-1-969615-03-0

All rights reserved.

Published by As You Wish Publishing

connect@asyouwishpublishing.com

No portion of this book may be reproduced in any form without written permission from the publisher or author, except as permitted by U.S. copyright law.

Contents

Introduction

These stories are not meant to be read quickly.

They come from a tradition where wisdom was passed in simple scenes, short conversations, and moments that did not announce themselves as important. A farmer answering a question. A teacher waiting before speaking. Someone noticing where they are standing.

Many of these stories have been told in different forms for hundreds of years. They survive because they do not demand agreement. They invite attention.

What you will find here are original retellings and contemplative reflections inspired by that lineage. They are not instructions. They are not answers. They are small mirrors, held at different angles, offering another way to look.

Some stories may feel familiar. Others may not land at all. That is part of the design. These teachings were never meant to be consumed all at once or understood the same way by everyone.

You can read one story and close the book. You can return later. You can skip around. Nothing is lost by doing so.

If there is a common thread, it is this: life rarely reveals its meaning on our timetable. Much of what matters unfolds slowly, without commentary.

These stories do not try to speed that up. They simply point, and then step aside.

Maybe

The farmer lived just beyond the last paved road, where the town thinned into fields and the days were shaped more by weather than by clocks. His house was modest, worn smooth by years of wind and sun. He had one good field, a small orchard, and a single horse he relied on to plow and haul what the land would give.

One morning, before the kettle had finished heating, he noticed the pasture gate standing open. The rope that usually held it shut had slipped loose in the night. The horse was gone.

By midday, word had traveled. Neighbors stopped by under the pretense of concern, though curiosity carried them just as much.

"That's terrible luck," one said. "You depend on that horse," said another. "Without it, the season will be hard."

The farmer listened. He did not argue. He did not agree. He stood looking out at the empty field, as if waiting for something else to arrive.

"Maybe," he said.

A few days passed.

Early one morning, dust rose on the road. The farmer stepped outside and saw his horse returning, unhurried and calm. Behind it followed two others, younger and strong, drawn along by whatever invisible agreements animals make with one another.

By afternoon, the neighbors returned.

"This changes everything," they said. "How fortunate," they said. "Your luck has turned."

The farmer watched the horses settle into the field, the grass bending under new weight.

"Maybe," he said.

Later that week, his son tried riding one of the new horses. The animal startled, bolted, and threw him hard against the ground. The sound carried farther than the fall itself.

The boy's leg broke cleanly, but badly. Healing would take time.

Again, the neighbors came.

"This is awful," they said. "First the trouble, then the hope, and now this."

The farmer sat with his son through the long night, changing cloths, keeping watch. When the neighbors spoke, he nodded once.

"Maybe," he said.

Not long after, notices were posted in town. Young men were being called to serve. Officials went door to door, measuring bodies, checking names, making marks on lists that could not be undone.

When they reached the farmer's house, they saw the boy's leg bound and unmoving. They made no mark and moved on.

The neighbors returned one last time.

"That saved him," they said. "That injury protected him." "You were spared something worse."

The farmer stood at the edge of the field as evening settled in. The horses moved slowly now, grazing without urgency. The road lay quiet again.

"Maybe," he said.

We're trained to decide quickly. Good or bad. Gain or loss. Blessing or mistake.

The farmer does none of this.

He doesn't deny pain or relief. He just refuses to claim certainty while the story's still unfolding.

"Maybe" isn't passivity. It's restraint.

It's the discipline of not collapsing the future into the present just to feel safe.

When something goes wrong, we rush to name it. When something goes right, we rush again. But life doesn't move in straight lines, and meaning doesn't arrive on our schedule.

What looks like loss may interrupt a greater harm. What looks like fortune may carry unseen costs.

The farmer understands something quiet and difficult: Events aren't finished when they arrive.

"Maybe" leaves space for life to keep revealing itself. It keeps the heart open without pretending to understand. It lets us stay present without forcing a conclusion.

This isn't indifference. It's humility.

And in a world that demands immediate judgment, humility may be the deepest form of wisdom we have.

The Teacher and the Sweetness

A woman traveled some distance to see a teacher known for his clarity. When she arrived, she bowed and spoke plainly.

"I eat too much sugar," she said. "I know it isn't good for me, but I can't stop. Will you help me?"

The teacher listened without interrupting. When she finished, he nodded once.

"Come back in a week," he said. "Then I will help you."

The woman was surprised but didn't argue. She returned home and waited.

A week later, she came back as instructed. Again she bowed, and again she asked for help.

This time, the teacher didn't hesitate.

"Stop eating sugar," he said.

The woman blinked. She waited for more.

"That's it?" she asked. "That's it," he replied.

She hesitated, then asked the question that had been sitting with her all week.

"Why didn't you tell me that the first time I came?"

The teacher looked at her for a long moment before answering.

"Because last week," he said, "I was still eating sugar."

Advice travels easily. Practice doesn't.

The teacher doesn't delay because the answer is complicated. He delays because truth spoken without embodiment is hollow.

He knows that words carry weight only when they're lived. Otherwise, they're just sounds passing through the air.

Waiting a week isn't a strategy. It's integrity.

The teacher refuses to ask the woman to do something he hasn't faced himself. Not because he wants to be pure, but because he wants to be honest.

This story isn't about sugar. It's about alignment.

We sense, often without knowing how, when guidance is rooted in experience and when it's not. We feel the difference in our bodies.

What changes us isn't instruction. It's resonance.

And resonance only comes when someone has walked the path far enough to speak from inside it.

The Streetlight

L ate one evening, a man was walking home when he noticed a woman on her hands and knees beneath a streetlight. She was moving slowly, patting the ground, eyes fixed on the small circle of light cast onto the pavement.

Concerned, he stopped.

"Are you all right?" he asked. "I've lost my needle," she said, without looking up.

He set his bag down and knelt beside her. Together they searched, fingers tracing cracks in the concrete, brushing aside dust and leaves. Minutes passed.

They found nothing.

After a while, the man paused. "Where did you last have it?" he asked.

The woman stopped searching and looked up at him.

"In the house," she said. "Then why are you looking for it out here?" he asked.

She gestured toward the streetlight overhead.

"The light is better here," she said.

We often search where it's easiest to look. Not where the truth actually lives.

The streetlight offers clarity, visibility, comfort. The house is darker, more familiar, harder to navigate.

So we stay in the light.

We analyze problems where language is available. We seek answers where others can see us working. We circle ideas instead of entering the places that feel uncertain or private.

This isn't foolishness. It's human.

Looking inward requires a different kind of seeing. One that doesn't guarantee quick results or public reassurance.

The needle is rarely lost where we're most comfortable searching. It's usually left behind where attention slipped, where presence was thin, where we didn't want to stay long.

The story doesn't say the woman is wrong. It just reveals the cost of mistaking illumination for truth.

Light helps. But it can't replace honesty about where something was actually lost.

Sometimes the work isn't to brighten the search, but to return to the place we've been avoiding.

The Empty Cup

A scholar came to see a teacher whose presence was known to be quiet and precise. He arrived with questions already formed, arguments already rehearsed.

They sat together, and the teacher poured tea.

He filled the cup. And kept pouring.

Tea spilled over the rim, ran down the sides, pooled on the table.

The scholar laughed, startled. "It's full," he said. "You can't pour anymore in."

The teacher set the pot down.

"Exactly," he said.

We often come seeking understanding while already carrying answers.

We arrive filled with opinions, experiences, conclusions, identities. We want confirmation, refinement, reassurance.

But nothing new can enter a cup that's already full.

The teacher doesn't criticize the scholar. He doesn't argue. He just lets the tea speak.

Emptiness, in this story, isn't ignorance. It's availability.

To be empty is to pause certainty long enough for something else to appear. Not to discard what we know, but to loosen our grip on it.

Learning begins not when we accumulate more, but when we make space.

And space isn't created through effort. It's created through release.

The cup doesn't need to become better. It only needs to become open.

The Raft

A traveler came to a wide river just before dusk. The water moved fast and dark, swollen from recent rain. There was no bridge in sight, no easy crossing. The far bank was visible but distant, softened by mist.

The traveler waited. Night came.

By morning, the river hadn't changed.

He searched along the bank and found scraps left behind by others—broken boards, lengths of rope, pieces of bark. He gathered what he could and, over time, built a small raft. It was uneven and rough, but it floated.

He pushed off and crossed carefully, using his hands more than any tool. The current pulled at the raft, testing each joint. When he reached the far side, he was tired, soaked, and grateful.

He stepped onto land and pulled the raft with him.

As he continued his journey, the raft became a burden. It scraped against rocks, caught on roots, slowed his pace. Still, he carried it. He'd worked hard to build it. It had saved him once.

Others he met asked why he dragged it along.

"This raft helped me cross the river," he said. "It would be foolish to abandon it."

Farther on, the path narrowed. The terrain grew steep. Carrying the raft became nearly impossible.

Exhausted, the traveler finally stopped. He looked back at the river behind him, then forward at the road ahead.

The Sound of the Bell

A monastery sat above a village, close enough that the bell could be heard each morning and evening. Its sound marked the hours, steady and dependable.

A young student arrived one winter and began his training. He worked hard, followed instructions carefully, and watched the senior monks closely. Still, he felt restless. He wanted to understand something essential, something he couldn't yet name.

One evening, as the bell rang, he went to the teacher.

"I hear the bell every day," the student said. "Yes," the teacher replied.

"But sometimes it sounds clear, and sometimes it feels distant," the student continued. "The bell is the same. Why does it change?"

The teacher didn't answer. Instead, he asked the student to walk with him.

They went outside, down the stone steps, and stood near the bell tower. The air was cold. The bell rang again, loud and full.

Then the teacher led the student farther away, down the path toward the trees. The bell rang once more, thinner now, softened by distance.

They kept walking. By the time the bell rang again, it was barely audible.

The teacher stopped.

"Has the bell changed?" he asked.

The student shook his head. "No," he said.

"What changed, then?" the teacher asked.

The student listened to the fading sound and didn't answer.

They walked back in silence.

We often believe clarity comes and goes on its own.

We say we're connected one day and distant the next. Focused in one moment, scattered in another. Certain now, confused later.

But the bell keeps ringing.

What changes is our position.

Attention moves closer or farther away. Presence narrows or opens. We drift without noticing and then blame the sound for fading.

The teacher doesn't explain this with words. He lets the body understand first.

Nothing's wrong with the bell. Nothing's broken in the silence.

Sometimes what we're seeking hasn't left us at all. We've simply wandered.

And the path back isn't effort or correction. It's listening, and noticing where we're standing now.

The Gate

A traveler reached a monastery at the end of a long road. His feet were sore, his pack worn thin. He'd heard the teacher there spoke plainly and didn't waste words.

At the entrance stood a simple wooden gate. It wasn't locked. Still, the traveler hesitated.

A monk sweeping nearby paused and watched him.

"I've come to study," the traveler said. "Then enter," the monk replied.

"But am I ready?" the traveler asked. "I don't know enough yet."

The monk leaned on his broom. "What do you think is on the other side of the gate?" he asked.

"Understanding," the traveler said. "Peace," he added after a moment.

The monk nodded and returned to sweeping.

The traveler stood there for a long time. He adjusted his pack, straightened his clothes, rehearsed questions he might ask. The gate didn't move.

Finally, tired of standing, he stepped forward.

The gate swung open easily.

We often wait for readiness before beginning.

We want certainty before commitment, understanding before entry. We believe there's a threshold that must be crossed internally before we're allowed to step forward.

The gate, in this story, doesn't test the traveler. It doesn't demand proof.

It waits.

Readiness is rarely something we achieve in advance. It arrives through movement, not preparation.

The traveler doesn't become ready by standing still. He becomes ready by entering.

Many gates in life remain open and unused because we keep circling them, asking questions instead of stepping through.

The gate opens naturally, not because of readiness.

The Long Road

A student and his teacher set out early one morning, walking toward a town the student had never seen. The road was wide at first, then narrowed, winding through fields and low hills.

After some time, the student slowed.

"How far is the town?" he asked.

The teacher looked ahead, then back at the student. "We'll see," he said.

Not long after, they met a woman walking in the opposite direction. The student stopped her.

"Excuse me," he said. "How far is the town from here?"

She smiled. "Just a couple of miles," she said, and continued on her way.

The student nodded and walked on, relieved.

A while later, they came upon a man resting by the side of the road.

"How much farther to the town?" the student asked.

"Not far," the man said. "Just a short way."

The road stretched on. The sun rose higher.

Again, the student asked someone they passed. "Just a couple of miles," came the answer.

This happened again and again. Each time, the student felt both encouraged and confused. The town never seemed closer, yet the answers never changed.

Finally, as evening approached, the student stopped.

"Teacher," he said, "everyone keeps telling me it's only a couple of miles away. Yet we've been walking all day. Why does no one say how far it truly is?"

The teacher stopped with him and rested his pack on the ground.

"If I had told you at the beginning that the journey would take many days," he said, "would you have started?"

The student was quiet.

"No," he admitted.

The teacher nodded.

"I knew the distance," he said. "But you needed the road in pieces."

They walked on.

Some journeys are too large to be taken all at once.

If we could see their full length from the beginning, we might turn away, overwhelmed before the first step. So the path reveals itself gradually.

The teacher doesn't deceive the student. He protects the beginning.

Having already walked the road, the teacher knows the terrain. He knows when to speak and when to stay quiet. His patience isn't indifference—it's care.

Progress isn't always made by seeing the whole picture. Often it's made by taking the next small distance we can bear.

Those who've already traveled far learn something: people move forward more reliably through encouragement than through magnitude.

The road is long. But it's walkable.

And sometimes wisdom lies not in revealing the destination, but in helping someone take the next few steps without fear.

The Clearing

A teacher and a student were traveling through unfamiliar land when night fell faster than expected. The forest closed in around them, thick with undergrowth and sound. Animals moved unseen. The path beneath their feet was narrow and uneven.

The student grew anxious.

"We shouldn't keep going," he said. "We can't see."

The teacher didn't answer. He walked slowly, feeling the ground with each step.

A storm moved in. Wind bent the trees. Rain came down hard, then stopped as suddenly as it had begun.

Clouds thinned and thickened again, shifting across the sky.

At one point, the moon broke through.

For a brief moment, the forest floor was visible. Roots, stones, the faint outline of the trail ahead appeared and then dimmed again.

The student lifted his head, searching the sky, waiting for the moon to return.

The teacher kept walking.

Another break in the clouds came. This time, the teacher noticed where the light fell. He saw the next few steps, then the next bend, then a small clearing just ahead.

He led them forward while the student remained behind, still watching the sky.

When the student finally caught up, they were standing safely in the clearing.

"How did you know where to go?" the student asked.

"I didn't look for the light," the teacher said. "I looked for what the light revealed."

It's easy to mistake the source of insight for the work itself.

The student watches the sky, waiting for something dramatic to appear again. He's drawn to the light, to the moment of illumination, to the thing that feels powerful and reassuring.

The teacher watches the ground.

He knows that insight isn't meant to be admired. It's meant to be used.

Teachers, teachings, moments of clarity, even profound awakenings—they're like brief openings in the clouds. They show us what's already here. They don't walk the path for us.

Fixating on the teacher keeps the eyes lifted away from the road. Following the path takes attention, humility, and movement.

Wisdom isn't something to stare at. It's something to step into.

The light comes and goes. The path remains.

The Broken Handle

A student was sent each morning to draw water from the well. The bucket was old, its wooden handle worn smooth from years of use. The student noticed a thin crack forming where the handle met the rim.

He brought the bucket to the teacher.

"It will break," the student said. "Yes," the teacher replied.

"Should we replace it now?" the student asked. "No," the teacher said. "Use it."

Days passed. The crack widened. Each morning the student carried the bucket carefully, adjusting his grip, moving slower than before.

One morning, halfway back from the well, the handle finally snapped. The bucket tipped, water spilling into the dirt.

The student stood there, holding the broken handle, ashamed.

"I should have insisted," he said. "Now the water is gone."

The teacher came to where he stood.

"The water returned to the ground," the teacher said. "And the handle showed you where it was weak."

They gathered the bucket, repaired it, and returned to the well together.

We often want to fix things before they fail.

We sense weakness and rush to remove it, replace it, erase it. We believe strength comes from preventing breaks.

But some understanding arrives only through use.

The teacher doesn't ignore the crack. He allows the student to feel it in his hands.

Carrying something fragile teaches attentiveness. It slows us down. It reveals where care is needed.

When the handle breaks, nothing essential is lost. The water returns. The bucket can be mended. What remains is knowledge that couldn't have been learned in advance.

Not every flaw needs immediate correction. Some need to be carried until they teach us how to hold things differently.

Breakage is instruction, not failure.

The Unfinished Fence

A farmer was repairing a fence along the edge of his field. The work was simple but long, stretching farther than he could complete in a single day.

A student passing by stopped to watch.

"You've left a section undone," the student said, pointing to the far end.

"Yes," the farmer replied.

"Won't the animals get through?" the student asked.

"Not today," the farmer said, tightening a post.

The student stayed, uneasy. He watched as the farmer packed up his tools while the fence still stood incomplete.

"Why not finish it now?" the student asked. "There's still light."

The farmer wiped his hands and looked at the field.

"Because if I hurry to finish," he said, "I will do it poorly. And if I wait until tomorrow, I will see the fence more clearly."

The next morning, the farmer returned. Overnight, nothing had crossed the open section. In the clear light of day, he noticed a place where the ground dipped. He adjusted the fence there, making it stronger than before.

We often believe completion is the same as care.

We push to finish, to close the loop, to make something whole before it's had time to reveal what it needs.

The farmer knows that stopping is part of the work. Rest creates perspective. Distance sharpens attention.

Leaving something unfinished isn't neglect. It can be trust.

Some things improve when given space. Some mistakes only become visible after we step away.

Patience isn't delay for its own sake. It's respect for timing.

The fence holds because it was done properly, with the time and attention needed.

The Weight of the Stone

A student carried a stone in his pack wherever he went. It was smooth and heavy, chosen careful ly from the riverbed near the monastery.

At first, the weight reminded him of his practice. Each step felt deliberate. Each movement mattered.

Over time, the stone became familiar. The student stopped noticing it, though his shoulders grew sore and his pace slowed.

One day, while resting by the path, the teacher sat beside him.

"You walk as if you are tired," the teacher said.

"I am," the student replied. "But this stone helps me remember what matters."

The teacher nodded and reached into the student's pack. He lifted the stone, turned it in his hands, and placed it gently on the ground.

"Sit," he said.

They sat in silence.

After a while, the teacher stood and began walking again. The student followed, forgetting for a moment about the stone.

When he realized the pack was lighter, he stopped.

"My stone," he said.

The teacher turned back.

"You remembered without it," he said.

The stone remained by the path, warming in the sun.

What supports us at one stage can become unnecessary later.

We cling to reminders, rituals, symbols, believing they're what hold our understanding in place. We fear that without them, meaning will slip away.

But understanding matures.

The stone doesn't disappear because it was wrong. It's set down because it's no longer needed.

Carrying weight can teach strength and focus. Setting weight down teaches trust.

Practice isn't measured by what we carry, but by what we've integrated.

When the reminder has done its work, it can rest.

And we can walk on, lighter, without forgetting.

The Rain

A merchant arrived at an inn late in the evening, drenched and irritable. Rain had followed him for three days, turning the roads to mud and delaying his journey.

Inside, he found a monk sitting by the fire, drying his robes.

"This rain," the merchant said, shaking water from his cloak. "It's ruined everything. My goods are soaked. I've lost time. I've lost money."

The monk looked up briefly, then back at the fire.

"Yes," he said. "It's been raining."

The merchant sat down heavily. "You don't seem bothered by it."

"I got wet," the monk said.

"That's all?" the merchant asked. "You're not angry? Frustrated?"

The monk considered this. "The rain fell on me," he said. "I didn't argue with it."

The merchant stared at him. "But surely you wish it would stop."

"When it stops," the monk said, "it will have stopped."

They sat in silence for a while. The fire cracked. Outside, the rain continued, steady and indifferent.

The merchant shifted in his seat. "So you just accept it? No matter what happens?"

The monk tilted his head slightly. "I accept that it rained. What I do next is something else."

He stood, his robes nearly dry, and moved toward the door.

"Where are you going?" the merchant asked.

"To check the road," the monk said. "If it's passable, I'll walk. If not, I'll wait."

He opened the door. The rain had softened to a drizzle.

The monk stepped outside. The merchant sat by the fire a while longer, listening to the water drip from the eaves.

We add so much to what simply is.

The rain falls. We tell ourselves stories about what it means, what it's ruined, what it's stolen from us.

The monk doesn't pretend the rain isn't there. He doesn't pretend he isn't wet. But he doesn't carry the rain inside him either.

There's the event. And there's everything we pile on top of it.

Most of our suffering lives in that second part.

The rain doesn't care what we think of it. It falls or it doesn't. The road is passable or it isn't.

What remains is only this: what we do with what's in front of us.

Not what we wish were different. Not what we feared or hoped for.

Just this. Right here. Right now.

The Two Monks and the River

Two monks were walking back to their monastery when they came to a river swollen with recent rain. At the crossing stood a young woman in fine clothes, hesitant at the water's edge.

"Please," she said. "I need to cross, but the current is too strong."

The older monk didn't pause. He lifted her onto his back, waded through the rushing water, and set her down safely on the other side. She thanked him and went on her way.

The two monks continued walking.

An hour passed in silence. Then another.

Finally, the younger monk spoke.

"Brother," he said, "our order forbids us from touching women. Yet you carried her across the river."

The older monk looked at him.

"I set her down on the other side," he said. "Are you still carrying her?"

We carry things long after they've been set down.

A comment someone made. A mistake we can't undo. A moment that's already passed.

The older monk didn't pretend the rules didn't exist. He saw what was needed in that moment and acted. Then he moved on.

The younger monk followed the letter of the teaching but missed something deeper—he turned a brief crossing into hours of weight.

We do this constantly. We replay conversations. We grip old grievances. We hold onto what should have happened instead of what did.

The river is behind them. The woman is gone. But one monk walks freely while the other stumbles under invisible weight.

The question isn't whether we pick things up. We will. Life asks that of us.

The question is: do we know how to put them down?

The Master's Silence

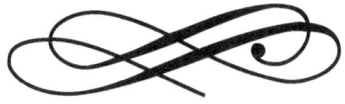

A renowned teacher grew old and frail. Word spread that he would soon die, and students came from distant places to hear his final wisdom.

They gathered in his room, filling every space, some standing in the doorway, others pressed against the walls. Notebooks ready. Hearts expectant.

The teacher lay still, his breathing shallow.

"Master," one student said softly, "please share with us what you've learned. We've traveled so far."

The teacher's eyes opened slightly. He looked at the faces surrounding him.

He said nothing.

Hours passed. Some students shifted uncomfortably. Others whispered to each other, wondering if he had the strength to speak.

As evening came, a young monk who had served the teacher for many years leaned close.

"Teacher," he said, "they're waiting for your final teaching."

The old man's lips moved. The room fell silent, everyone straining to hear.

"I'm dying," he whispered.

Then he closed his eyes and was quiet again.

One by one, the students left, confused and disappointed. They had expected something profound, something to write down and carry home.

Only the young monk remained.

In the middle of the night, the teacher stirred. The monk brought water to his lips.

"Did they understand?" the teacher asked.

"I don't think so," the monk said.

The teacher smiled faintly. "I gave them everything I had to give."

By morning, he was gone.

We wait for wisdom to arrive as words.

But sometimes the teaching is the moment itself, unadorned and complete.

The teacher didn't withhold anything. He showed them exactly what was happening—a man dying, present with his dying, neither running from it nor dressing it up.

No final philosophy. No clever summary. Just this: what's actually here.

The students wanted something to take with them, something to possess. They wanted wisdom packaged for the journey home.

The teacher gave them the only honest thing left—his presence in his final hours, undistracted by their need for meaning.

Most of us miss it too. We're so busy waiting for the profound moment that we overlook the one we're standing in.

The teaching isn't always hidden in the words. Sometimes it's breathing right in front of us, asking only that we see it as it is.

The Garden Wall

A young mason was hired to build a wall around the monastery garden. He worked carefully, selecting each stone, checking every angle with his level, making sure each row sat perfectly straight.

The abbot passed by each day but said nothing.

After two weeks, the wall was nearly complete. The mason stepped back to admire his work. Every stone was precisely placed. Every line was true.

The abbot came to inspect it.

He walked along the wall slowly, running his hand across the surface. Then he stopped at one section and pressed his palm against it.

"This part is too perfect," he said.

The mason frowned. "Too perfect? I don't understand."

The abbot gestured to the forest beyond the garden. "Look at those trees. Are they straight?"

"No," the mason said.

"Look at that stream. Does it run in a perfect line?"

"No."

"Then why should your wall?"

The mason looked confused. "But isn't quality in the precision? The evenness?"

The abbot picked up a small, irregular stone from the ground. He handed it to the mason.

"Build the wall so that it belongs here," he said. "Not so that it impresses visitors."

The mason held the stone, turning it in his hands. It was rough, asymmetrical, nothing like the carefully chosen stones he'd been using.

The next day, the abbot returned. The mason had removed several stones from the "too perfect" section and replaced them. The wall now had a slight, almost imperceptible curve. Some stones protruded slightly more than others. It looked less like a monument and more like something that had grown there.

"Better," the abbot said. "Now it breathes."

We often confuse perfection with life.

We chase the flawless angle, the polished surface, the thing that can't be criticized. We build to impress, to prove, to protect ourselves from judgment.

But perfection is rigid. It stands apart. It announces itself.

Life curves. It's uneven. It fits into the world rather than demanding the world accommodate it.

The mason wasn't doing bad work. His wall was technically excellent. But it was trying too hard. It had forgotten where it was.

Sometimes what we're making needs less control, not more. Less insistence on our vision, more listening to what's already there.

The wall doesn't serve the garden by dominating it. It serves by belonging to it.

And maybe we're the same. Maybe we become most useful not when we're perfectly constructed, but when we finally stop trying to be anything other than what this moment, this place, this life actually needs.

The Mountain Path

Two monks set out to climb a sacred mountain. Both had trained for years. Both carried the same provisions. Both started at dawn.

The first monk climbed steadily, his eyes fixed on the summit. When the path forked, he always chose the steeper route. When he grew tired, he pushed harder. Other pilgrims passed him going down, their faces peaceful, and he barely looked at them.

"Almost there," he told himself at each turn.

The second monk climbed slowly. He stopped often—to drink from a stream, to rest in the shade, to help an elderly woman adjust her pack. When the path forked, he sometimes chose the longer way because it passed through a grove of cedars.

A young girl sat crying by the trail, separated from her family. The second monk sat with her until her parents found her, then continued up.

By the time the sun began to set, the first monk reached the summit. He stood there, breathless and alone, looking out at the world below. He had imagined this moment for years.

He waited for something—some feeling of completion, some transformation.

The view was beautiful. But he felt hollow.

After a few minutes, he started back down. He had to reach the base before dark.

The second monk never made it to the top. By evening, he was only halfway up the mountain. He found a flat rock, laid out his mat, and watched the sunset paint the clouds.

A family camping nearby invited him to share their fire. He told stories. They laughed together. He fell asleep under the stars, the summit somewhere above him in the darkness.

The next morning, he woke early and continued down. He hadn't reached the top, but he wasn't bothered.

Years later, someone asked the first monk about climbing the sacred mountain.

"I made it to the summit," he said. But he couldn't remember much else about the journey.

They asked the second monk the same question.

"I never reached the top," he said. Then he smiled. "But I remember everything about that day."

We're taught that the point is to arrive.

To reach the summit, close the deal, finish the degree, hit the goal. We climb with our eyes up, measuring distance, counting progress.

And sometimes we make it. We stand at the top. We take the photo.

And then we realize the peak is just a place. It doesn't change us. It doesn't fill the hollow we thought it would.

The second monk didn't fail. He just understood something the first monk missed: the mountain isn't the summit. The mountain is every step, every person, every moment along the way.

You can spend your life chasing peaks and never actually live on the mountain.

The first monk conquered it. The second monk walked it.

One saw it as an obstacle between him and achievement. The other saw it as the thing itself.

We think we'll be happy when we arrive. But we're already here. This is it. This moment, this breath, this imperfect middle of things.

The summit will still be there tomorrow. Or it won't. Either way, the question isn't whether you reached it.

It's whether you were awake for the climb.

The Broken Bowl

A potter brought his finest bowl to the monastery as a gift. It had taken him months to create—the clay perfectly centered, the glaze rich and even, the form balanced and elegant.

The abbot accepted it with a bow and placed it on a shelf in the meditation hall where everyone could see it.

That evening, during cleaning, a young student accidentally knocked it to the floor. It shattered into dozens of pieces.

The student fell to his knees, horrified. Other students rushed over. Someone ran to find the abbot.

When the abbot arrived, he found the student still kneeling, surrounded by fragments, his face pale.

"Master, I'm so sorry," the student said. "It was so beautiful. I've ruined it."

The abbot knelt down beside him and picked up one of the larger pieces. He held it up to the lamplight, studying the glaze.

"Look at this," he said.

The student looked up, confused.

"See how the break revealed the layers?" the abbot continued. "The clay, the slip, the glaze. You can see how it was made now. Before, it was just a surface."

He set the piece down gently and picked up another.

"And this shape—I never would have imagined it. The break created something the potter never intended."

The student stared at the fragments scattered across the floor. "But it's destroyed."

"It's changed," the abbot said. "That's different."

Over the next few days, the abbot collected the pieces. He didn't throw them away or try to glue them back together. Instead, he placed several fragments in different parts of the monastery—one on the windowsill of the library, another in the garden beside a stone, a third near the entrance gate.

When the potter returned weeks later and saw a piece of his bowl sitting among the rocks in the garden, weathered now by rain, he stopped.

"My bowl," he said to the abbot, who was nearby.

"Yes," the abbot replied. "It serves better now."

The potter looked at the fragment for a long time. Then he smiled.

"I spent months trying to make something permanent," he said.

"You succeeded," the abbot said. "Just not in the way you planned."

We grieve what breaks as if wholeness were the only form of value.

But breaking isn't the same as ending.

The bowl didn't become worthless when it shattered. It became something else—more honest, maybe. More integrated into the life of the place.

We spend so much energy trying to keep things intact. Our plans. Our identities. Our ideas about how things should be. And when they break, we think we've failed.

But sometimes the breaking is what lets something breathe. What lets us see what was hidden. What allows a thing to finally stop performing and just exist.

The student saw destruction. The abbot saw transformation.

Neither was wrong. But only one could move forward.

We're all broken bowls in one way or another. The question isn't whether we'll shatter—we will. The question is whether we'll let the pieces find new purpose, or spend our lives trying to glue together something that was never meant to stay the same.

The Student's Question

A student had been at the monastery for three years. He meditated daily, worked in the gardens, studied the texts, and followed every instruction carefully.

One morning, he approached his teacher with frustration written across his face.

"Master," he said, "I've practiced exactly as you've taught. I wake early. I sit in silence. I watch my breath. But nothing has changed. I feel the same as when I arrived."

The teacher was tending to a small pine tree, carefully trimming away dead needles.

"Come with me," he said.

They walked to the edge of the monastery grounds where a massive oak tree stood, its branches spreading wide overhead.

"Do you see this tree?" the teacher asked.

"Yes," the student said.

"How tall is it?"

The student looked up. "Maybe forty feet."

"When I first came here," the teacher said, "this tree was barely taller than you are now."

The student studied the thick trunk, the sprawling limbs. "That must have taken decades."

"It did," the teacher said. "Now tell me—on which day did it become tall?"

The student opened his mouth, then closed it.

"Was it the day the roots first pushed deeper? The spring when the branches stretched toward the sun?

The winter when it stood bare but growing still beneath the surface?"

The student looked down at his feet.

"I don't know," he said quietly.

"Neither does the tree," the teacher replied. "It simply continues."

They stood together in the shade. Above them, leaves moved in the wind, the sound like distant water.

"You think you should feel different," the teacher said. "But the person who arrived three years ago would not have asked this question. He would not have noticed his own impatience. He would not have stood here listening."

The student looked at the tree again, seeing it differently now.

"Growth is happening," the teacher said, returning to the path. "You're just too close to notice."

We expect transformation to announce itself.

We think we should feel it happening—some dramatic shift, some clear before and after. When we don't, we assume we're doing it wrong.

But most growth is silent. Invisible. It happens in increments too small to measure on any given day.

The tree doesn't stop to evaluate its progress. It doesn't compare itself to other trees or worry that it's not growing fast enough. It just grows.

We're the same, except we interrupt ourselves constantly with measurement. With judgment. With the belief that if we can't see change, it isn't happening.

But the person asking "am I growing?" has already grown beyond the person who never thought to ask.

The work isn't to manufacture some visible transformation. It's to keep showing up. To keep sitting. To keep breathing. To keep doing the small, unremarkable things that roots do in the dark.

One day you'll look back and realize you're not standing where you used to be.

But there won't be a single moment when it happened.

Just a thousand quiet mornings that became a life.

The Two Students

Two students arrived at the monastery on the same day. Both were young, earnest, and eager to learn.

The first student asked the master, "How long will it take me to reach enlightenment?"

"Ten years," the master said.

The student's face fell. "Ten years? That's so long. What if I work twice as hard? What if I practice day and night?"

The master considered this. "In that case," he said, "twenty years."

The student looked confused but said nothing more.

The second student asked nothing. He simply bowed and went to find his room.

Years passed.

The first student practiced intensely. He rose before everyone else. He sat longer. He studied more texts. During meals, he barely ate, anxious to return to meditation. When others rested, he continued.

He kept track of his progress in a journal. He noted every insight, every moment of clarity, every sign that he was advancing toward his goal.

The second student woke with the bell. He sat when it was time to sit. He worked in the kitchen, swept the halls, mended his robes when they tore. He laughed with the other monks. He sometimes fell asleep during evening meditation.

Ten years passed.

One morning, the master called both students to his room.

To the first student, he said, "You have worked harder than anyone I've taught. Your dedication is remarkable."

The student bowed, waiting.

"But you are further from understanding now than when you arrived."

The student's face went pale. "How is that possible? I've done everything. I've sacrificed everything."

"Yes," the master said. "That's the problem. You've been so busy trying to reach enlightenment that you forgot to live."

He turned to the second student.

"And you—you asked for nothing. You expected nothing. You simply showed up each day."

The second student looked surprised. "I often felt I wasn't trying hard enough."

"Trying to grab water makes it slip through your fingers," the master said. "You cupped your hands and let it come to you."

The first student stood rigid, his jaw tight. "So I wasted ten years?"

"No," the master said gently. "But now you have a choice. You can spend the next ten years angry about the first ten. Or you can finally begin."

Striving can become its own obstacle.

The first student wasn't lazy or uncommitted. He was desperate. And desperation, no matter how disciplined it looks, is just fear wearing different clothes.

He kept score. He measured. He white-knuckled his way toward something he thought he could force into existence.

The second student didn't do less—he just did it differently. He wasn't chasing. He was present.

There's a difference between discipline and grasping. Between commitment and clinging.

One moves with life. The other fights it.

We think more effort always equals more progress. But sometimes more effort just means we're squeezing tighter, trying to control what can only unfold.

The things worth finding don't come because we chase them harder.

They come because we finally stop running and notice they've been here all along.

The Mirror

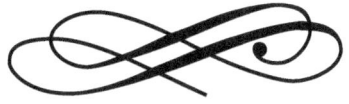

A wealthy merchant heard of a master whose wisdom was said to be unmatched. He traveled for weeks to find him, bringing an expensive gift—a mirror framed in silver, polished to perfection.

When he arrived, the master was sitting in a bare room, sunlight falling through a single window.

The merchant bowed and presented the mirror. "Master, I've come seeking truth. I've brought this gift as an offering."

The master accepted it and held it up, studying his reflection.

"What do you see when you look in this?" the master asked.

"I see myself," the merchant said.

The master nodded and set the mirror down. Then he stood and walked to the window. He gestured for the merchant to join him.

"And when you look through this?" the master asked.

The merchant looked out. "I see people. The village. Children playing. A woman carrying water."

"Interesting," the master said. "Both are made of glass. One shows you only yourself. The other shows you the world. What's the difference?"

The merchant thought for a moment. "The mirror has a coating of silver on the back."

"Yes," the master said. "A thin layer of silver, and suddenly you can see nothing but your own face."

He picked up the mirror again and handed it back to the merchant.

"You brought me a gift," the master said. "But perhaps you should keep it. Look into it each day. And ask yourself: how much silver is covering your window?"

The merchant held the mirror, seeing his own confused expression staring back.

"I don't understand," he said.

"You came here seeking truth," the master said. "But you cannot see it while you're standing in your own way."

He returned to his seat. "When you're ready to look through the window instead of at the mirror, come back."

The merchant left, carrying the mirror with him.

Years later, he returned. The mirror was gone—he'd left it behind somewhere along the road. He couldn't remember when.

The master was still sitting in the same room, older now, the sunlight falling the same way.

"I'm ready to look through the window," the merchant said.

The master smiled. "You already are."

We spend most of our lives looking at mirrors.

Measuring ourselves. Comparing. Adjusting our image. Consumed with how we appear, what we've achieved, whether we're enough.

The silver coating is thin—just our accumulated ideas about who we are, what we deserve, what we need to protect.

But it's enough to block out everything else.

The window is right there. Same glass. Same light. But we can't see through it while we're busy studying our reflection.

Letting go of the mirror doesn't mean hating yourself or denying who you are. It just means turning around. Remembering there's a whole world that exists beyond your own image.

Most wisdom traditions say the same thing in different words: get out of your own way.

Not by force. Not by shame. Just by noticing how much energy goes into maintaining the reflection, and asking if maybe, just once, you could look through the glass instead.

The world is already there, waiting.

It's been there the whole time.

The Fire

A monastery sat high in the mountains, built over generations by monks who had lived there for centuries. Its library held ancient texts. Its gardens had been tended for lifetimes. Every stone in its walls had been placed with care.

One night, a fire started in the kitchen. By the time anyone noticed, flames had spread to the main hall.

The monks formed lines, passing buckets of water from the well. But the fire moved faster than they could. The abbot stood watching, his face illuminated by the orange glow.

A young monk ran to him, frantic. "Master, the library! We have to save the texts!"

"The texts are burning," the abbot said calmly.

"But they're irreplaceable!" the monk shouted over the roar of flames. "Centuries of wisdom!"

The abbot didn't move. "Keep passing water," he said. "Stay away from the walls."

The young monk stared at him in disbelief, then ran toward the library anyway. Two older monks caught him and held him back.

By dawn, half the monastery was gone. The library, the meditation hall, the abbot's quarters—all reduced to ash and blackened timber.

The monks stood in silence, exhausted, faces streaked with soot.

The young monk who had wanted to save the texts sat on the ground, his head in his hands. "We lost everything," he said.

The abbot sat down beside him. Together they watched smoke rise into the pale morning sky.

"What did we lose?" the abbot asked.

"The teachings," the young monk said. "The scrolls. The building our founders built."

"The scrolls held words," the abbot said. "Do you remember any of them?"

The young monk nodded slowly. "Some."

"Then they're not lost." The abbot gestured to the other monks scattered around the courtyard. "Do they remember?"

"Yes."

"The building gave us shelter. But we're still here. Are we still monks without those walls?"

The young monk looked at his brothers, at the abbot, at the well they'd drawn water from all night.

"Yes," he said quietly.

"Then what did we lose?" the abbot asked again.

The young monk was silent for a long time. Finally, he said, "Our attachment to it."

The abbot smiled. "Now you understand why I didn't run into the fire."

Weeks later, as they cleared the rubble, the young monk found a partially burned text. Only a few pages remained legible. He brought it to the abbot.

"Look," he said. "Something survived."

The abbot glanced at it. "Good. We can use the paper to start the cooking fire."

The young monk hesitated, then laughed. He understood.

They rebuilt, but differently. The new library was smaller. The walls simpler. And when visitors came and asked about the fire, the monks spoke of it not as a tragedy, but as a teaching.

We confuse what holds the truth with the truth itself.

The books weren't the wisdom. The building wasn't the practice. They were just containers, and containers can break.

The young monk wanted to preserve something he thought was essential. But what's essential can't burn.

It lives in how we carry ourselves, what we remember, who we are when everything else is stripped away.

Loss teaches us what's real.

Not by taking something away, but by showing us what remains when everything removable is gone.

The abbot didn't give up. He didn't stop being a teacher when his library burned. He just stopped pretending that wisdom lived in objects instead of people.

We all have fires. Relationships end. Careers collapse. Plans turn to ash. Health fails. People die.

And we stand there watching, convinced we're losing everything that matters.

But if the truth you carry can be destroyed by fire, it wasn't truth. It was just something you were holding.

What matters walks out of the flames with you.

Everything else is just smoke.

The Bridge

A monk spent twenty years building a bridge across a deep gorge. The canyon separated two villages, and crossing it required a full day's dangerous journey down one side and up the other.

He worked alone, mostly. Sometimes villagers would help, bringing stones or timber, but the monk was there every day, in all weather, laying foundation, raising supports, testing each beam.

People thought he was crazy at first. Then admirable. Then they stopped thinking about him at all. He was just part of the landscape—the monk building his bridge.

After twenty years, the bridge was finished.

It was beautiful. Solid. The two villages celebrated. Children ran across it laughing. Merchants used it to trade goods. Families reunited.

The monk stood at one end, watching people cross, his hands rough and scarred from decades of work.

A young traveler stopped beside him. "You must be proud," she said. "Twenty years of your life, and now look—everyone benefits."

The monk nodded but said nothing.

"Will you cross it?" she asked.

"No," the monk said.

"Why not? You built it."

"I built it so others could cross," he said. "I don't need to. I've been on both sides already."

The traveler looked confused. "Then what was the point? All that work, and you won't even use it?"

The monk smiled. "I used it every day for twenty years," he said. "Each stone I placed, each measurement

I checked—that was my crossing. The bridge was just what remained."

He picked up his worn tools and simple pack.

"Where will you go now?" the traveler asked.

The monk looked down the road. "I hear there's another gorge," he said. "Three days' walk from here. No bridge yet."

"You're going to build another one?"

"Maybe," the monk said. "Or maybe I'll just help someone else build theirs."

He bowed to the traveler and walked away, leaving his bridge behind.

We think the point is the thing we make.

The book. The business. The family. The career. The accomplishment.

But those are just the evidence of how we spent our time. The residue of our crossing.

The real work happens in the building. In showing up each day. In placing one stone and then another, even when no one's watching, even when progress is invisible.

The monk didn't need the bridge. He needed the twenty years of building it.

That's where he lived. That's where he learned whatever he learned. The bridge was just the path he walked while becoming whoever he became.

We get confused because we're taught to chase outcomes. To measure success by what we produce, what we finish, what we can point to.

But the person who finishes isn't the same person who started. And that transformation—quiet, unmarked, impossible to photograph—that's the actual prize.

The bridge will stand there whether the monk crosses it or not.

He's already somewhere else, because building it carried him there.

The work isn't about the work. It's about who you become while doing it.

Everything else is just what you leave behind for others to use.

The Sandal

A student noticed that his teacher wore the same pair of sandals every day. They were old, the leather cracked and worn thin in places, the straps mended multiple times with rough cord.

One day, the student's family sent him money. He went to the village and bought a fine new pair of sandals—soft leather, sturdy soles, elegant stitching. He presented them to his teacher.

"Master, please accept these. Your sandals are falling apart."

The teacher looked at the new sandals, then at his old ones.

"Thank you," he said, and set the new pair in the corner of his room.

The next day, the teacher wore his old sandals.

And the next day. And the day after that.

Weeks passed. The new sandals sat untouched. The old ones grew more tattered.

Finally, the student's frustration broke through. "Master, why won't you wear the sandals I gave you? Don't you like them?"

"They're beautiful," the teacher said.

"Then why?"

The teacher sat down and gestured for the student to sit as well.

"Tell me," the teacher said, "why did you buy them?"

"Because yours are worn out."

"And why does that bother you?"

The student hesitated. "Because... because a teacher should look respectable. Because people might think we don't take care of you. Because—"

He stopped.

The teacher waited.

"Because it bothers me to see them," the student said quietly.

"Ah," the teacher said. "So the gift was for you, not for me."

The student felt his face flush. "I wanted to help."

"I know," the teacher said gently. "But help that comes from discomfort with what is—that's not help. That's management of your own unease."

He held up one of his sandals. "These have walked with me for years. They've shaped to my feet. They know the path. When they can no longer serve, I'll replace them. But that's my discernment to make, not yours."

"But they're falling apart," the student said.

"Yes," the teacher agreed. "Many things fall apart. Should we rush to fix them all before their time?"

Three months later, the strap on the teacher's sandal finally broke completely, beyond repair. That evening, he unwrapped the new sandals and put them on.

The student saw him wearing them the next morning.

"They fit well," the teacher said, smiling. "Thank you. The timing is right now."

We give gifts to quiet our own discomfort.

We see something that bothers us—a person's choices, their worn possessions, their way of living—and we call the feeling "care." We rush to fix, to improve, to make things match our idea of how they should be.

But care that can't tolerate what is isn't really care. It's control dressed in kindness.

The student wasn't wrong to notice. He wasn't wrong to offer. But he couldn't sit with the teacher's old sandals. He needed them to change so he could feel better.

Real generosity has space in it. It offers without insisting. It sees a need and responds, but doesn't require the response to look a certain way.

The teacher knew his sandals. He knew when they still served and when they didn't. The student only knew his own discomfort.

Sometimes the most loving thing we can do is nothing. Just witness. Just allow. Just trust that others know their own lives better than we do.

The gift that comes from genuine care doesn't need to be used immediately to have value.

It waits. It's patient. It trusts timing that isn't ours to decide.

The Seed

A woman came to the monastery carrying her child. The boy was still, wrapped in cloth, his small face peaceful as if sleeping.

She found the teacher in the garden and fell to her knees.

"Please," she said. "Bring him back. They say you have power. They say you can heal. Please."

The teacher looked at the child, then at the woman's face, hollow with grief.

"I can help you," he said. "But first, you must bring me something."

Hope flickered in her eyes. "Anything. Tell me what you need."

"A mustard seed," he said. "But it must come from a home that has never known sorrow."

The woman stood immediately. "I'll find it."

She went to the first house at the edge of the village. An old man answered.

"Please," she said, "I need a mustard seed from a home that has never known sorrow."

The old man's face softened. "Come in," he said. "I have mustard seeds. Take as many as you need."

She stepped inside, and he gestured to a chair where a shawl lay folded.

"My wife's," he said. "She died last winter."

The woman touched the shawl, then shook her head. "I cannot take a seed from this house."

She went to the next home. A young couple lived there with three children, who were playing in the yard.

"Has this house known sorrow?" she asked.

The woman of the house glanced at the her alter of flowers. "An illness ran through our family taking my mother and my sister."

The grieving mother moved on.

House after house, the same. A son lost to war. A father who drank. A daughter who left and never returned. A business that failed. An illness that wouldn't end. A marriage that broke. A hope that died.

She walked all day. Then another day. And another.

Each home had mustard seeds. Each home had sorrow.

By the time she returned to the monastery, dusk was settling. She no longer carried her child—she had buried him that morning, in a place overlooking the valley.

The teacher was still in the garden.

She stood before him, her hands empty.

"I couldn't find a home without sorrow," she said.

"No," the teacher said gently.

"So you cannot help me."

"I already have."

She looked at him, tears finally coming. "My son is still gone."

"Yes," he said. "And you are no longer alone in that."

She sank to the ground, and this time when she wept, it was different. The grief was still there, as heavy as before. But it was no longer a wall separating her from the world.

It was a thread connecting her to every house she'd visited, every face that had softened with recognition, every door that had opened.

"What do I do now?" she whispered.

The teacher sat beside her. "You walk back through the village. And when you see someone carrying what you carry, you'll know. And they'll know you know."

Grief wants to believe it's unique.

That our loss is deeper, our pain more isolating, our wound beyond what others could understand.

And in one sense, it's true. No one else lost your child, your parent, your love, your dream. The specifics are yours alone.

But the weight? That's universal.

The teacher didn't diminish her loss. He didn't say "everyone suffers, so get over it." He sent her out to discover something she couldn't be told: that sorrow is the ground we all walk on.

She didn't find a house without grief. She found that grief is the price of love, the cost of being alive, the thing that makes us most human.

The mustard seed couldn't bring her son back. But it brought her back—to the world, to the village, to the communion of those who've lost and still keep living.

We think healing means the pain goes away. Sometimes it just means we stop carrying it alone.

The thread that connects us isn't joy. Joy separates—my happiness, your happiness, maybe they never touch.

But sorrow? Sorrow is the place where every wall comes down.

Where we finally see each other as we are.

Breakable. Loving. Still here.

Conclusion

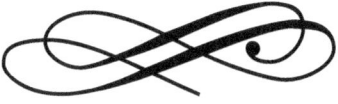

At some point, stories stop being about the characters in them.

The farmer no longer belongs to the field. The teacher no longer belongs to the monastery. The road is no longer somewhere else.

What remains is the quiet recognition that much of life does not need to be resolved in order to be lived.

Zen stories have endured not because they offer certainty, but because they make room. They loosen our grip on the need to decide too quickly, to arrive too soon, to be finished before we are ready.

If you have reached the end of this book, nothing is required of you. There is no lesson to summarize or insight to carry forward like a possession.

Perhaps one image stayed with you. Perhaps one line surfaced at an unexpected moment. Perhaps nothing did, and that is fine too.

The work of these stories does not happen on the page. It happens later, in ordinary moments. While waiting. While walking. While listening to something familiar in a new way.

The book can close here.

The path does not.

www.ingramcontent.com/pod-product-compliance
Lightning Source LLC
Chambersburg PA
CBHW071524120626
46550CB00006B/2352